BREAD + CHEESE

YES, PLEASE!

ISBN-13: 978-1-56383-626-8
Item #7152

**Printed in the USA
by G&R Publishing Co.**

Distributed By:

507 Industrial Street
Waverly, IA 50677

www.cqbookstore.com

gifts@cqbookstore.com

 CQ Products

 CQ Products

 @cqproducts

 @cqproducts

GIVE YOUR SANDWICH SOME ATTITUDE... THE MORE, THE BETTER!

Forget exact measurements and lengthy instructions, these simple "recipes" leave room for you to get creative with your sandwiches. After all, aren't rules meant to be broken?

Simple ingredient lists make it easy to create your own variations. If you LOVE avocado, then pile on avocado; if you hate mustard, leave it off – the choice is yours. So layer it up, spice it up, or sweeten it up... any way you toast it, we're taking this classic sandwich to a whole new level.

Here are a few tricks of the grilled cheese sandwich trade.

Preheating is the key to a crispy sandwich: Make sure to preheat your cooking surface before placing your sandwich on it. This will guarantee a crispy outside.

Keep those fillings inside: Try using larger slices of meats and vegetables, as opposed to small pieces. This will help prevent the fillings from tumbling out of the sandwich.

Consider the veggies: Make sure to remove excess moisture from vegetables before adding them to your sandwich by patting them dry with a paper towel. If you prefer fresh veggies as opposed to cooked, you can leave them off during cooking and add them right before serving, giving a fresh crunch to your sandwich!

Nobody likes a soggy sandwich: It's best to add sauces and spreads to the sandwich just before cooking so they don't have as much time to seep into the bread.

Thickness is key: There's nothing wrong with overstuffing your grilled cheese, but keep in mind the inner-most ingredients will take longer to get warm. Make sure you cover your pan to keep as much heat as possible around your sandwich.

It's all about personal preference, so decide what you like and roll with it!

MAKE MAGIC HAPPEN

Anybody can make a good sandwich, but follow a few tips and yours will be out of this world!

Start with a Good Base

Look for sturdy bread that will hold up well. Sourdough, French, and Italian are reliable, but be bold and try something new. Pretzel and ciabatta rolls, bagels, and even donuts are fun choices.

Add Great Cheese

For super-flowy, melty cheese, try Brie, mild cheddar, Gouda, and Havarti, to name a few. If you like a nice pull and stretch, add cheese curds, mozzarella, or Monterey Jack for instance. Experiment to find your fave.

Give it Some Guts

Give your sandwich personality and make it your own by piling on what you like. Meat (from the deli or leftovers from your fridge), fresh fruits or veggies, even pasta (if that's your thing) are all wonderful choices.

Bring on the Extras

That's what gives the finished sandwich that little somethin'-somethin' that takes it over the top. Throw on some condiments, herbs, and spices to turn a great sandwich into a spectacular one.

GREEN TORPEDO

INGREDIENTS

Jalapeños, sliced lengthwise, seeds & membranes removed

Cream cheese, softened

Italian bread slices, one side buttered

Sharp cheddar, sliced

Monterey Jack, sliced

Bacon, crisp-cooked

Fresh cilantro, chopped

Stuff jalapeños with cream cheese and bake for 25 minutes at 375°. Layer ingredients between bread slices and toast both sides.

COBB SALAD, HOLD THE LETTUCE

INGREDIENTS

Whole wheat bread slices,
one side buttered

Boneless, skinless chicken
breast, cooked & sliced

Bacon, crisp-cooked

Avocado, sliced

Egg, hard-cooked & sliced

Gouda, shredded

Blue cheese crumbles

*Layer ingredients
between bread slices
and toast both sides.*

BIG FAT GREEK SANDWICH

INGREDIENTS

Original flavored hummus
Sourdough bread slices,
 one side buttered
Provolone, sliced
Red onion, sliced
Deli-sliced roast turkey
Roasted red peppers, sliced
Cucumber, sliced
 Kalamata olives, sliced
  Feta crumbles

*Spread hummus on the
unbuttered side of the
bread. Layer remaining
ingredients between slices
and toast both sides.*

SPAGHETTI BOAT

INGREDIENTS

Italian bread slices,
   one side buttered &
   sprinkled with garlic salt

Prepared spaghetti with sauce

Romano, shredded

Italian seasoning

Layer all ingredients between bread slices and toast both sides.

MIGHTY MUFFALETTA

INGREDIENTS

Sourdough bread slices,
  one side buttered
Provolone, sliced
Mozzarella, sliced
Deli-sliced Genoa salami
Deli-sliced ham
Giardiniera, chopped
Green olives, sliced
Kalamata olives, sliced
  Pepperoncini, sliced

*Layer ingredients
between bread slices
and toast both sides.*

STUCK IN A JAM

INGREDIENTS

White bread slices,
  one side buttered
Cream cheese, softened
Strawberry jam
Strawberries, sliced
Honey
Fresh mint

*Spread the cream cheese
and jam on the unbuttered
side of the bread. Layer
remaining ingredients
between slices and toast
both sides.*

THE CORDON BLEU

INGREDIENTS

Sourdough bread slices,
one side buttered

Mayo

Dijon mustard

Boneless, skinless chicken
breast, cooked & sliced

Thinly sliced prosciutto

Gruyère, shredded

Fresh thyme

Combine the mayo
and mustard. Layer all
ingredients between bread
slices and toast both sides.

THE 'Q CREW

INGREDIENTS

Boneless, skinless chicken breast, cooked & shredded

Barbecue sauce

Sourdough bread slices, one side buttered

Red onion, sliced

Provolone, sliced

Fresh cilantro, chopped

Combine the shredded chicken and barbecue sauce. Layer all ingredients between bread slices and toast both sides.

THE BEEFCAKE

INGREDIENTS

Red onion, sliced
Balsamic vinegar
Salt
Mayo
Prepared horseradish
Multigrain bread slices,
 one side buttered
Fresh baby spinach
 Deli-sliced roast beef
  Blue cheese crumbles

Sauté the onion; remove from heat and add the vinegar and salt. Combine the mayo and horseradish and spread on the unbuttered side of the bread. Layer all ingredients between slices and toast both sides.

HEY, HEY, WHAT D'YA CAPRE·SAY

INGREDIENTS

Boneless, chicken breast
Garlic powder
Italian seasoning
Black pepper
Italian bread slices,
  one side buttered
Mozzarella, shredded
Tomato, sliced
Fresh basil, chopped

Cook chicken in a skillet and season with garlic powder, Italian seasoning, and pepper. Layer all ingredients between bread slices and toast both sides. Serve with balsamic glaze for dipping.

THE PEACHY-KEEN

INGREDIENTS

Ciabatta roll, split &
  outsides buttered

Whole grain Dijon mustard

Peach preserves

Canadian bacon slices

Peach, sliced

Fontina, shredded

Fresh thyme

Spread mustard and peserves on the inside of the roll. Layer remaining ingredients between roll halves and toast both sides.

FRESH FROM THE GARDEN

INGREDIENTS

Cream cheese, softened

Fresh chives, chopped

Red onion, finely chopped

Whole wheat bread slices, one side buttered

Variety of tomatoes, sliced

Fresh basil, shredded

Salt & pepper

Combine the cream cheese, chives, and onion and spread the mixture on the unbuttered side of the bread. Layer remaining ingredients between slices and toast both sides.

NACHO REGULAR GRILLED CHEESE

INGREDIENTS

Cheese bread slices,
  one side buttered
Pepper Jack, sliced
Black beans, drained & rinsed
Black olives, sliced
Green onion, sliced
Avocado, sliced
Salsa
  Nacho cheese tortilla chips

Layer ingredients
between bread slices
and toast both sides.
Serve with sour cream
for dipping.

THE RANGOON SWOON

INGREDIENTS

Cream cheese, softened
Green onion, sliced
Garlic salt
Soy sauce
Worcestershire sauce
Black pepper
Sourdough bread slices,
   one side buttered
Cooked shrimp

Combine cream cheese, green onion, garlic salt, soy sauce, Worcestershire sauce, and black pepper and spread on the unbuttered side of the bread. Add the shrimp and toast both sides.

PACK ON THE POUND (CAKE)

INGREDIENTS

Pound cake slices,
   one side buttered

Dark chocolate bar

Brie, sliced

Raspberries

*Layer ingredients
between cake slices
and toast both sides.*

LIVIN' ON A GRUYÈRE

INGREDIENTS

Multigrain bread slices,
  one side buttered

Mayo

Crisp red apple, thinly sliced

Gruyère, shredded

Fresh arugula

*Spread mayo on the
unbuttered side of the
bread. Layer remaining
ingredients between slices
and toast both sides.*

SUCH A GOUDA MUSHROOM

INGREDIENTS

Portobello mushrooms, sliced
Garlic, minced
Cream cheese, softened
Sourdough bread slices,
    one side buttered &
    sprinkled with garlic salt
Fresh baby spinach
Gouda, shredded
Fresh chives, chopped
    Salt & pepper

*Sauté the mushrooms
and garlic. Spread cream
cheese on the unbuttered
side of the bread. Layer all
ingredients between slices
and toast both sides.*

THE PORT OF TURKEY

INGREDIENTS

Sourdough bread slices,
  one side buttered

Port wine cheese spread

Provolone, sliced

Deli-sliced roast turkey breast

Tomato, sliced

Bacon, crisp-cooked

Black pepper

Spread the port wine cheese on the unbuttered side of the bread. Layer remaining ingredients and toast both sides.

THE LOX-STAR

INGREDIENTS

Everything bagel, split &
  one side buttered

Cream cheese, softened

Gruyère, sliced

Nova lox

Red onion, sliced

Capers

Fresh dill

*Spread cream cheese on
the unbuttered side of the
bagel. Layer remaining
ingredients between bagel
halves and toast both sides.*

FIELD OF GREENS

INGREDIENTS

Multigrain bread slices,
   one side buttered
Deli-sliced roasted turkey
Fresh arugula
Avocado, sliced
Goat cheese, crumbled

*Layer ingredients
between bread slices
and toast both sides.*

DON'T YOU FORGET ABOUT BRIE

INGREDIENTS

Sourdough bread slices,
  one side buttered

Brie, sliced

Thinly sliced prosciutto

Fresh arugula

*Layer ingredients
between bread slices
and toast both sides.*

THE FRENCHMAN

INGREDIENTS

6″ French bread loaf,
   split & one side buttered

Gruyère, sliced

Deli-sliced ham

Sweet gherkins, sliced

Dijon mustard

Dried tarragon

Black pepper

*Layer ingredients
between bread halves
and toast both sides.*

THE OKTOBER-FEAST

INGREDIENTS

Pretzel roll, split &
  outsides buttered

Muenster, sliced

Honey mustard

Brat, cooked & sliced
  in half lengthwise

Coleslaw

Caraway seed

*Layer ingredients
between roll halves
and toast both sides.*

I LOVE BROC & ROLL

INGREDIENTS

Ciabatta roll, split &
   outsides buttered

Sharp cheddar, sliced

Honey mustard

Deli-sliced smoked
   turkey breast

Broccoli, steamed

Salt & pepper

*Layer ingredients
between roll halves
and toast both sides.*

THE BREAKFAST CLUB

INGREDIENTS

Raspberry jam
Multigrain bread slices,
  one side buttered
Provolone, sliced
Thinly sliced prosciutto
Deli-sliced roast turkey breast
Egg, cooked over easy
Fresh arugula
Black pepper

*Spread jam on the
unbuttered side of the
bread. Layer remaining
ingredients between slices
and toast both sides.*

GET TO THE MEAT & POTATOES

INGREDIENTS

Top sirloin steak

Yellow onion, sliced

Potato, thinly sliced

Salt & pepper

French bread slices, one side buttered & sprinkled with garlic salt

Provolone, sliced

Green onion, sliced

Cook and season the steak to your liking; thinly slice. Sauté onion and potato; season with salt & pepper. Layer all ingredients between bread slices and toast both sides.

THE CINNA-BLUE

INGREDIENTS

Cinnamon raisin bread
  slices, one side buttered

Mascarpone

Blueberries

Semisweet chocolate chips

Spread mascarpone on the unbuttered side of the bread. Layer remaining ingredients between bread slices and toast both sides.

PEAR ME THE DETAILS

INGREDIENTS

Fig jam

Multigrain bread slices, one side buttered

Cheddar, sliced

Bacon, crisp-cooked

Pear, thinly sliced

Spread jam on the unbuttered side of the bread. Layer ingredients between slices and toast both sides.

LET'S GUAC ABOUT IT

INGREDIENTS

Guacamole

Sourdough bread slices,
   one side buttered

Bacon, crisp-cooked

Colby Jack, shredded

Tortilla chips, crumbled

*Spread guacamole on the
unbuttered side of the
bread. Layer ingredients
between bread slices
and toast both sides.*

HOLY STROMBOLI!

INGREDIENTS

6" French bread loaf,
   split & one side buttered
Pizza sauce
Mozzarella, sliced
Deli-sliced Genoa salami
Deli-sliced Capicola ham
Red onion, sliced
Pepperoncini, sliced ⟿

Sun-dried tomatoes
Parmesan, shredded

*Spread pizza sauce on
the unbuttered side of the
bread. Layer remaining
ingredients between slices
and toast both sides.*

DELECTABLE DESSERTS

Who said grilled cheese sandwiches are just for lunch? Keep these sweet tips in mind when creating a dessert grilled cheese sandwich!

Cheese Choices

Don't overlook the importance of the cheese! Mascarpone and cream cheese are obvious choices for dessert, but brie and Muenster also pair well with a little sweetness.

RECIPE PAGE 11

Sweet as Honey

If you're still looking for a little extra sweetness, honey is an easy fix. Try mixing honey with mascarpone or cream cheese to kick up the sweetness. A small drizzle can go a long way!

RECIPE PAGE 43

Bold Breads

Switching out normal bread for a unique version is an easy way to transform a grilled cheese into a sweet treat. Try substituting pound cake, cinnamon raisin bread, banana bread, or even donuts.

RECIPE PAGE 20

Flavorful Fillings

Fillings are the star of a dessert grilled cheese. Chocolate, fruit, peanut butter, and marshmallows are all great choices. We combine all four in our Funky Monkey sandwich.

RECIPE PAGE 38

THE FUNKY MONKEY

INGREDIENTS

Cream cheese, softened
Creamy peanut butter
Chocolate hazelnut spread
Banana bread slices,
   one side buttered
Banana, sliced
Mini marshmallows

Spread the cream cheese, peanut butter, and chocolate hazelnut on the unbuttered side of the bread. Layer remaining ingredients between slices and toast both sides.

WHY SO SLOPPY, JOE?

INGREDIENTS

Ground turkey, chicken, beef, or pork

Barbecue sauce

Sourdough bread slices, one side buttered

American cheese, sliced

Plain wavy potato chips

Dill pickles

Cook the ground meat until browned. Add the barbecue sauce and let simmer. Layer all ingredients between bread slices and toast both sides.

IT'S CRUNCH TIME

INGREDIENTS

Sourdough bread slices,
  one side buttered

Sharp cheddar, sliced

Tomato slices

Barbecue potato chips

Pickled jalapeños

Bacon, crisp-cooked

*Layer ingredients
between bread slices
and toast both sides.*

THE REUBEN REUNION

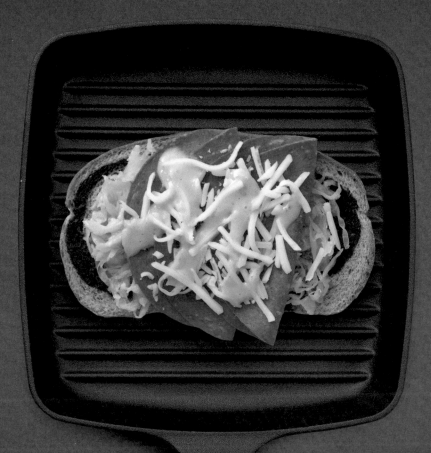

INGREDIENTS

Marble rye bread, one side buttered

Sauerkraut, drained

Deli-sliced corned beef

Swiss cheese, shredded

Thousand Island dressing

Layer ingredients between bread slices and toast both sides.

STRUTTIN' ON HOLE-Y GROUND

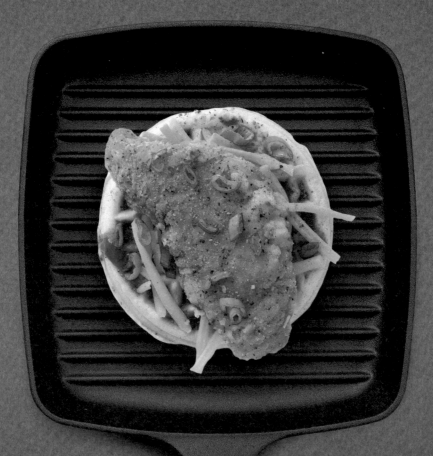

INGREDIENTS

Frozen waffles, thawed &
   one side buttered

Hot sauce

Sharp cheddar, shredded

Breaded chicken tenders,
   cooked

Cajun seasoning

Green onions, sliced

Layer ingredients between waffles and toast both sides. Serve with honey or maple syrup for dipping.

APPLE PIE IN THE SKY

INGREDIENTS

Mascarpone

Honey

Cinnamon raisin bread
slices, one side buttered

Crisp green apple,
cored & thinly sliced

Brown sugar

Combine the mascarpone and honey and spread on the unbuttered side of the bread; add the apples and a little brown sugar. Sprinkle the outside of the sandwich with more brown sugar and toast both sides. Top with vanilla ice cream.

EVERY DAY I'M BRUSSELIN'

INGREDIENTS

Brussels sprouts, stems
   removed & thinly sliced

Garlic, minced

Salt & pepper

Balsamic vinegar

Whole grain bread slices,
   one side buttered

Havarti, sliced

*Sauté the Brussels sprouts
and garlic; add salt, pepper,
and balsamic vinegar.
Layer all ingredients
between bread slices and
toast both sides.*

BELLA, BELLA, SMOKY FELLA

INGREDIENTS

Baby Bella mushrooms, sliced

Cream cheese, softened

6" French bread loaf, split
   & one side buttered

Chipotle peppers in
   adobo sauce, sliced

Cheddar, shredded

Fresh cilantro, chopped

*Sauté mushrooms.
Spread the cream cheese
on the unbuttered side
of the bread. Layer all
ingredients between halves
and toast both sides.*

THE FARMHAND

INGREDIENTS

Egg, cooked over easy

English muffin bread slices, one side buttered

Fresh baby spinach

Sharp cheddar, sliced

Bacon, crisp-cooked

Layer ingredients between bread slices and toast both sides.

PANCETTA MAC ATTACK

INGREDIENTS

Italian bread slices, one
  side buttered & sprinkled
  with garlic powder

Prepared macaroni
  & cheese

Pancetta, pan-fried

Asiago, shredded

*Layer ingredients
between bread slices
and toast both sides*

LET'S HAVE A LUAU

INGREDIENTS

Pizza sauce

Texas toast slices,
one side buttered

Deli-sliced ham

Pineapple rings

Mozzarella, shredded

Pickled jalapeños

*Spread the pizza sauce on
the unbuttered side of the
bread. Layer remaining
ingredients between slices
and toast both sides.*

THE BUFFALO RANCH

INGREDIENTS

Sourdough bread slices,
   one side buttered

Buffalo sauce

Provolone, sliced

Breaded chicken tenders,
   cooked

Ranch dressing

Blue cheese crumbles

Fresh chives, chopped

*Layer ingredients
between bread slices
and toast both sides.*

GO FOR THE PESTO!

INGREDIENTS

6" French bread loaf,
  split, one side buttered

Basil pesto

Mozzarella, sliced

Avocado, sliced

Deli-sliced roast turkey

Tomato, sliced

Black pepper

*Layer ingredients
between bread slices
and toast both sides.*

CHEESE TO THE NTH DEGREE

INGREDIENTS

Italian bread slices, one
    side buttered & sprinkled
    with shredded Parmesan

Provolone, sliced

Fresh mozzarella, sliced

Fontina, shredded

Cheese curds

*Layer ingredients
between bread slices
and toast both sides.*

JACK & DILL

INGREDIENTS

Sour cream

Mayo

Sourdough bread slices,
   one side buttered

Deli-sliced corned beef

Dill pickle relish

Dill-flavored Monterey
   Jack cheese, shredded

Green onion, finely chopped

Mix equal amounts of
sour cream and mayo
and spread on the
unbuttered side of the
bread. Layer remaining
ingredients and toast
both sides.

THE HEART OF THE MATTER

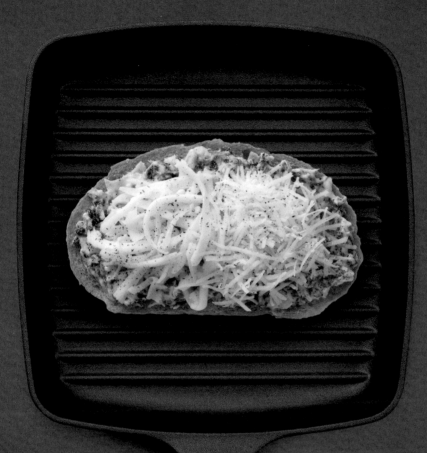

INGREDIENTS

Frozen chopped spinach
Canned artichoke hearts
Mayo
Garlic powder
Salt & pepper
Mozzarella, shredded
Parmesan, shredded
Sourdough bread slices,
  one side buttered

Thaw and squeeze excess moisture from the spinach and drain and chop the artichokes. Mix equal parts spinach, artichokes, and mayo; season with garlic powder, salt, and pepper and spread on unbuttered side of bread. Add cheeses and toast both sides.

THE GOOD LUCK PARM

INGREDIENTS

Marinara sauce

Sourdough bread slices, one side buttered

Breaded chicken tenders, cooked & sliced

Mozzarella, shredded

Parmesan, shredded

Fresh basil

Black pepper

Spread marinara sauce on the unbuttered side of the bread. Layer remaining ingredients between slices and toast both sides.

SUPERB CHIPOTLE & HERB

INGREDIENTS

Mayo

Lime juice

Chipotle chili powder

Salt & pepper

Pretzel roll, split & outsides buttered

Garlic & herb flavored Boursin cheese

Deli-sliced roast beef ⤳

Red onion, sliced

Radishes, thinly sliced

Dried rosemary

Mix mayo, lime juice, chili powder, salt, and pepper; spread on the unbuttered of the roll. Layer remaining ingredients between roll halves and toast both sides.

FRENCH TOAST OF THE TOWN

INGREDIENTS

Eggs, milk, vanilla,
  cinnamon & nutmeg
Butter
Thick-cut Italian bread slices
Egg, scrambled
Frozen hash browns, cooked
Brie, sliced
Bacon, crisp-cooked
Salt

Combine first five ingredients. Melt butter in skillet. Dip one side of a bread slice in egg mixture and place in the skillet. Layer remaining ingredients and top with another dipped bread slice. Toast both sides. Serve with maple syrup for dipping.

THE HOT POTATO

INGREDIENTS

Potato, sliced

Salt & pepper

Garlic powder

Sour cream

Texas toast slices,
   one side buttered

Cheddar, shredded

Bacon, crisp-cooked

Fresh chives, chopped

Fry potato slices; season with salt, pepper, and garlic powder. Spread sour cream on the unbuttered side of the bread. Layer all ingredients between slices and toast both sides.

DO-NOT JUDGE ME

INGREDIENTS

Maple-frosted donut,
   sliced in half & inside
   buttered

Bacon, crisp-cooked

Muenster, sliced

*Layer ingredients
between donut halves
and toast both sides.*

THE FEISTY FAJITA

INGREDIENTS

Red onion, sliced
Bell peppers, sliced
Zucchini, thinly sliced
Fajita seasoning
Queso fresco chipotle
  cheese wedge
Chimichurri sauce
Potato bread slices,
  one side buttered
Pepper Jack, sliced

Sauté veggies; stir in seasoning. Spread cheese wedge and chimichurri on unbuttered side of bread. Layer all ingredients between slices and toast both sides.

OPPOSITES ATTRACT

INGREDIENTS

Red pepper jelly

Italian bread slices, one side buttered

Deli-sliced smoked turkey breast

Brie, sliced

Strawberries, sliced

Fresh basil

Spread the jelly on the unbuttered side of the bread. Layer the remaining ingredients between slices and toast both sides.

THE CUBAN FUSION

INGREDIENTS

Sourdough bread slices,
   one side buttered

Swiss cheese, sliced

Shredded cooked pork roast

Canadian bacon slices

Dill pickles, sliced

Yellow mustard

*Layer ingredients
between bread slices
and toast both sides.*

LET'S GET SAUCY

Does a grilled cheese sandwich NEED a dipping sauce? Of course not. But you can never have too much sauce! These versatile sauce recipes are sure to add an extra kick to your sandwich creations.

Chipotle Mayo

In a blender or food processor, blend ½ C. mayo , ¼ C. sour cream, 2 peppers from a can of chipotles peppers in adobo, and the juice of 1 lime until finely chopped.

SANDWICH PAGE 4

Creamy Honey Mustard

Stir together ¼ C. mayo, 2 T. honey, 1 T. yellow mustard, 1 T. whole grain Dijon mustard, and 2 T. barbecue sauce.

SANDWICH PAGE 26

Sriracha Soy Ketchup

Stir together 1 C. ketchup, 2 T. brown sugar, 2 T. soy sauce, and 1 ½ tsp Sriracha sauce.

SANDWICH PAGE 17

SANDWICH PAGE 31

Chimichurri Sauce

In a blender or food processor, blend ½ C. each fresh parsley, fresh cilantro, olive oil, and red wine vinegar, ¼ C. chopped onion, 3-4 cloves minced garlic, 1 tsp. dried oregano, and ½ tsp. each salt and crushed red pepper until finely chopped.

INDEX

DIPPING SAUCES